Nature's Wild™

BIRDS OF PREY

by
Rebecca L. Grambo

Scientific Consultant:
MaryBeth Garrigan
The Raptor Center
St. Paul, MN

Published by Advance Publishers
www.advance-publishers.com

Contents

BIRDS THAT PREY

Birds of prey are meat-eating birds that use their strong feet to catch and kill prey. They also have strong, hooked beaks for tearing into flesh. Birds of prey are sometimes called raptors.

The bald eagle.

SHE'S BIGGER

Unusual among birds, raptor females are generally bigger than males. In some species, such as the little sparrowhawk (left), the female may be twice as big. Other raptors show less difference. Among species of vultures, males and females are about the same size.

DAY ▶ AND NIGHT

Most birds of prey are diurnal—active during the day. Most owls, however, are nocturnal. They do their hunting at night, relying on their hearing and low-light vision to locate prey.

SIMPLY BIRDS

Many birds, like the heron at right, eat other animals. But they are not called birds of prey, because they do not have the same kind of body or hunting methods that eagles, hawks, and other birds of prey do.

BIG AND ▲LITTLE

Raptors come in all sizes. Biggest of them all, the Andean condor (above) may weigh 25 pounds and have wings stretching to over 10 feet. It's about 250 times heavier than the smallest bird of prey, the tiny Asian falconet.

TOP OF THE HEAP

Raptors, such as this martial eagle, sit at the top of the food chain. Much like a lion, they hunt other animals, but almost nothing else hunts them. Their only enemies are other birds of prey and humans.

WEAK FEET

Vultures, such as this white-backed vulture, are considered birds of prey even though their feet are weak. Because vultures feed mainly on carrion (dead animals), lacking grasping power is not a big problem for them. Their beaks do all the work!

A HUNTER'S BODY

Birds of prey have a body suited for hunting other animals. From beak to tail feathers, every part serves a purpose.

A peregrine falcon.

▼FINE FEATHERS

Feathers do many jobs for birds of prey. Soft down keeps the birds warm. Strong feathers on the wings allow the birds to control flight. Tail feathers are used for steering and braking. The flight feathers on the wings of many owls, including this great horned owl, have a soft edge that makes flight noiseless.

TALONS OF DOOM▼

If you were a bird of prey, your toenails would be talons. A raptor's talon-tipped feet are its most important weapon. Some fish-eating raptors, such as this osprey, have specially curved claws and spiny bumps on their feet to help them hook and hang on to their wriggling catch.

▲NO CHEWING

Raptors, such as this Steller's sea eagle, have a big, strong beak that is great for tearing meat. But they don't have heavy teeth and jaws for chewing, because that would weigh them down. They do their chewing inside a part of the stomach called the gizzard. The gizzard's strong muscles contract around the food, grinding it against the rough inner surface to break it down.

WONDER WINGS ▼

Raptors that spend lots of time soaring have long, broad wings. By catching rising air currents, a bird like the turkey vulture (below) can cruise for hours and barely flap its wings. Soaring saves a lot of energy. Falcons, on the other hand, are fast-flapping flyers. Their narrow, pointed wings enable them to maneuver easily.

LIGHT BONES

To be able to fly well, birds of prey must weigh as little as possible. Hollow, air-filled bones are light but strong. Raptor skeletons are so light that in some species, such as the bald eagle, the bird's feathers weigh more than its bones!

EYE MOVEMENT

Raptor eyes are so big that they cannot move in their socket. The bird has to turn its whole head to look around. Raptors rely on their eyes and must avoid injuring them. A bony ridge above the eye gives some protection. Raptors also have a tough, partly transparent third eyelid that closes over their eyes to protect them when the birds are attacking prey or flying through branches.

EAGLE EYES

Birds of prey have eyesight that is at least two to three times better than ours. Some can see a grasshopper from a hundred yards away—the length of a football field! Eagles, such as the golden eagle (right), can spy rabbits and other prey from over a mile away.

GRABBING A MEAL

The ways raptors hunt are as varied as the foods they eat. Most hunt from the sky, but on occasion some will chase rabbits on foot through thick underbrush. The four-foot-tall secretary bird (below) prefers hunting on the ground. It walks in the grass of the African savannas looking for snakes. When it finds one, the secretary bird stomps on the snake to kill it.

TAKING THE PLUNGE ▲

The osprey is one of the few raptors to use this hunting technique: Soaring hundreds of feet above the water, looking for fish, it will tuck its wings in and dive as soon as it spots some prey. Just before hitting the water, it throws its wings back and plunges in feet first. Then it flaps out of the water with its catch.

10

◀ TEAMWORK

Most raptors hunt alone, but some hunt in pairs. Red-tailed hawks team up to capture gray squirrels. The one at left has caught a rat! However, only Harris's hawks hunt in family groups the way wolves do. As many as six may work in relays to chase prey.

PIRATE RAPTORS

Some raptors, including the African fish eagle (left), are aerial pirates. They annoy other birds carrying food, until the food is dropped. Then the pirate bird either catches the food in mid-air or picks it up from the ground. African fish eagles rob ospreys, herons, and even each other.

WHERE THERE'S FIRE

For many birds of prey, wildfires mean food. The birds gather to catch insects and other animals fleeing from the flames. Flocks of fifty to a hundred crested caracaras have been spotted feeding near the edge of grass fires.

▼SWEET LARVAE

Honey-buzzards go searching for bee and wasp nests. They dig the nests out of the ground, and eat the insects and honey. Their favorite bits seem to be the larvae—newly hatched, immature insects—which the honey-buzzards pick up one by one. Short, stiff feathers help protect the birds from being stung on the face.

SIT & WAIT ▲

The most common way that birds of prey hunt is to sit and wait for something to happen. This Harris's hawk has chosen a perch that gives it a good view. It will watch very carefully for prey, then quickly swoop down to make its catch.

▲ LOW & SLOW

Raptors often cruise back and forth close to the ground searching for their next meal. They look for movement and listen for the tiny sounds made by a scurrying mouse, vole, or other prey.

11

HOME, SWEET HOME

Birds of prey live on every continent except Antarctica. They may hunt over rain forest, desert, mountain, or prairie. Some raptors make long migrations each spring and fall, following food supplies and warm weather.

A Steller's sea eagle in Japan scans the water for prey.

IN THE RAIN FOREST

A chunk of South American rain forest may be home to more than fifteen raptor species, including large birds of prey, such as the harpy eagle (right). The lush and varied food supply makes the rain forest an ideal habitat. The harpy eagle hunts sloths, monkeys, and other animals that make their home in the treetops.

These red-tailed hawks have made their nest in a saguaro cactus in Arizona.

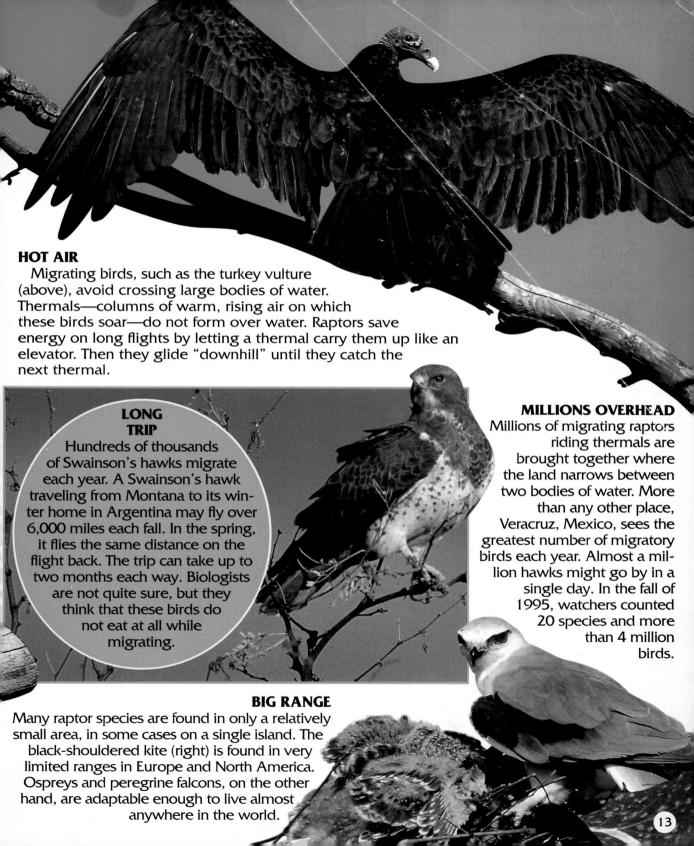

HOT AIR

Migrating birds, such as the turkey vulture (above), avoid crossing large bodies of water. Thermals—columns of warm, rising air on which these birds soar—do not form over water. Raptors save energy on long flights by letting a thermal carry them up like an elevator. Then they glide "downhill" until they catch the next thermal.

LONG TRIP

Hundreds of thousands of Swainson's hawks migrate each year. A Swainson's hawk traveling from Montana to its winter home in Argentina may fly over 6,000 miles each fall. In the spring, it flies the same distance on the flight back. The trip can take up to two months each way. Biologists are not quite sure, but they think that these birds do not eat at all while migrating.

MILLIONS OVERHEAD

Millions of migrating raptors riding thermals are brought together where the land narrows between two bodies of water. More than any other place, Veracruz, Mexico, sees the greatest number of migratory birds each year. Almost a million hawks might go by in a single day. In the fall of 1995, watchers counted 20 species and more than 4 million birds.

BIG RANGE

Many raptor species are found in only a relatively small area, in some cases on a single island. The black-shouldered kite (right) is found in very limited ranges in Europe and North America. Ospreys and peregrine falcons, on the other hand, are adaptable enough to live almost anywhere in the world.

MAKING A NEST

Raising a family is a big part of a raptor's life. Some species, such as bald eagles (left), may use the same nest for generations, adding to it each year. One nest was found to measure 10 feet wide and 20 feet deep, and weighed nearly 2 tons! In many species, the female decides the location for a new nest, and often does the building. The male brings in construction materials.

MATES

Many raptor mates stay together for a number of breeding seasons. When making courtship flights, some fly in big swoops as high up as 1,000 feet, then dive down. Others fly together as pairs, one above the other. The bird underneath rolls over in mid-flight to touch talons with the bird above. Bald eagles grab each other's talons and cartwheel downward.

A fuzzy, day-old eastern screech owl waits for its nest mates to hatch.

A LOT OF EGGS

Most diurnal birds of prey lay one to six eggs, depending on the species. Snowy owls sometimes lay a dozen! But raptors don't lay all their eggs at once. They wait a day or two after each egg before laying the next. The first chick to hatch is bigger than the others, and may kill its nest mates, especially if food is scarce. By eliminating competition, the chick ensures its survival.

Ferruginous hawks make their nest in the grasslands of the western U.S., where they may lay two to six eggs.

Just weeks after hatching, raptors begin to molt, growing their juvenile feathers. This four-week-old golden eagle, still partially downy, attempts a defensive posture.

14

AIRBORNE

The period of time lasting from the day a chick hatches from its egg to the day it takes its first flight is called the fledgling period. It may be as short as 23 days for small birds of prey, and as long as 130 days for large eagles. Condors have the longest fledgling period—up to 150 days.

▲ This young bald eagle is exercising its wings.

GO, DAD! ▶

From just before the eggs are laid until about midway through the nesting period, most male raptors are very busy providing food. Once males bring the food to the nest, it is up to the females to tear off pieces for the chicks.

FALCONS

Fast, fast, fast—that's the best way to describe falcons. With their long, pointed wings, they can really zip! Some specialize in catching birds.

FAST & ▶ DEADLY

The peregrine does its hunting in the air, swooping or diving down onto its prey with incredible speed—nearly 200 miles per hour—and delivering a killing blow with the hind talon protruding from its closed feet. Normally cliff-nesting birds, peregrine falcons have adapted to nesting in cities. Large populations of rock doves (pigeons) keep them well fed.

BIG & LITTLE ▶

Two feet tall with a five-foot wingspan, the gyrfalcon (right) is the largest and probably fastest falcon. It often captures prey by surprise, either "binding to it" (grabbing it in mid-air) or stunning it and returning to catch the prey as it falls. The smallest falcon, the sparrow-sized black-thighed falconet, is also the smallest of all raptors.

◀ DANGEROUS MEETINGS

Even among falcons, it is a rare feat to capture and kill a bird flying in the opposite direction. Only the lanner falcon (left) displays the coordination and timing needed to pull off a "head-on" kill.

▼ YUM, ROADKILL

Not as speedy as their falcon relatives, caracaras do most of their hunting on the ground, scavenging for whatever they can find. Often described as clever birds, caracaras may steal food from campers. Others have learned to cruise the highways at dawn to find whatever may have been hit and killed by cars during the night.

HOVERCRAFT

Falcons known as kestrels hunt by kiting, or hovering, over one spot. They do this by flying very slowly into the wind, balancing their speed with the wind's. When they spot prey, they dive hundreds of feet to make the kill.

◀ The robin-sized American kestrel is one of the smallest falcons.

PLAN AHEAD

Many falcons cache, or store, extra food, which gives them something to fall back on if prey is scarce. They stash food in a variety of places, including hollow trees, rain gutters, and switchboxes on utility poles.

KITES & HARRIERS

Although they're not very fast fliers, kites are graceful in the air. Harriers, like the one below, hunt by flying slowly close to the ground. Because their feet and legs are weaker than those of other hawks, kites and harriers hunt small mammals, frogs, snakes, and insects.

◀ The Brahminy kite, which ranges from India to Australia, preys on frogs, crabs, fish, and insects.

SNAIL ▶ SNACKS

Florida's snail kite is a snail specialist, eating no other prey. Its long, curved bill allows it to pull the snail from its shell. A snail kite's feeding perch can be identified by the pile of empty shells that lies beneath it.

18

LISTEN, LISTEN

The northern harrier is the only day-flying bird of prey in North America with sound-focusing facial discs. These discs, formed by feathers arranged like a shallow bowl, capture the slightest sounds. The harrier can find vole nests hidden in tall grasses by listening for the rodents' squeaks.

MID-AIR MEALS▼

The swallow-tailed kite doesn't wait to land before eating its food. All prey, including insects, snakes, and lizards, are consumed in mid-air. This kite has even been observed snatching up a whole nest and then, while still in flight, eating the young birds within, one by one.

LUNCH PASS

When a male harrier has food to give to his mate and their chicks, he doesn't always just take it to the nest. Sometimes he calls the female to fly out and meet him. Then he flies above her and drops the food. She catches it in her talons and takes it back to the nest while the male resumes hunting.

▲ LOW LIFE

Harriers often make their nests on the ground, hidden among tall grasses or reeds. After she builds the nest, the female lays her eggs. She usually lays only three or four, but if there's plenty of food around she may lay as many as ten.

BIRDS OF A FEATHER ▲

Birds of prey most often fly together when they migrate. Small raptors, such as kites, form flocks to gain information about where to find insects and other small prey.

HAWKS & BUZZARDS

Because of their short, rounded wings, most hawks are quick and able to maneuver through wooded areas when chasing prey. Buzzards are quite similar to hawks, and are sometimes called hawks, especially in North America. Buzzards tend to have longer, wider wings and shorter tails than hawks, and they are better suited for open country.

▼ The black-collared hawk, found in Central and South America, preys on fish, grasping its catch with feet specially equipped with spines.

◀ **WILD EYES**
When they are small chicks, Cooper's hawks have gray eyes. By the time they are a year old, their eye color has changed to a bright yellow. From then on, their eyes will gradually darken, becoming orange, then finally red.

DEADLY & DETERMINED
The goshawk dives into thick brush and scrambles over branches in pursuit of prey. It can weave through the forest at high speed, and often takes squirrels, rabbits, and birds by surprise.

CONFUSED? ▶

The most common buzzard in North America is called the red-tailed hawk. If that's not confusing enough for you, red-tails often fill in for eagles on TV and in the movies. The red-tailed hawk's screaming call is used in place of the bald eagle's creaky cackle.

◀ **IN BETWEEN**

Harris's hawk has a hawklike shape but buzzardlike behavior. This unusual raptor likes to use the top of a giant saguaro cactus as a hunting perch, and it often builds its nest in the saguaro's branches.

NO PERCH NEEDED ▲

The ferruginous hawk, actually a buzzard, prefers to hunt in open areas. It may hover while hunting ground squirrels and rabbits. Or it may just land and hunt from the ground, even if perches such as fence posts and telephone poles are nearby.

21

EAGLES

There are about 60 species of eagles living around the world. The smallest, the Nias serpent-eagle, has a wingspan of about three feet. The huge harpy eagle has a wingspan of about eight feet and weighs nearly 20 pounds—almost twice as much as a bald eagle.

SALMON FEAST▼

Although eagles are usually solitary, big food supplies can draw a crowd. Between October and December, as many as 3,000 eagles may gather in the trees along the Chilkat River in Alaska. The eagles feed on dead and dying salmon that have spawned in the river.

A cat snake is easy prey for the crested serpent-eagle.

BIG & STRONG

Africa's biggest eagle, the martial eagle (left), has a wingspan of about eight feet and may weigh as much as 13 pounds. It can kill small antelopes and jackals. Quite a bit smaller, the crowned hawk-eagle takes similar-sized prey and is known as Africa's most powerful eagle.

SNAKE SNACKS ▲

Snake-eagles and serpent-eagles prey on snakes almost exclusively. The short-toed snake-eagle often swallows its catch whole, leaving just the tail hanging out. If the eagle has a hungry chick to feed, it returns to the nest. The youngster grabs the tail and pulls, neatly retrieving the snake from the adult.

◄ FRUIT, PLEASE

The rather weird palm-nut vulture looks like a cross between a vulture and an eagle. Its diet is also unusual, because it prefers palm fruit to meat, eating other food, such as crabs and shellfish, only occasionally.

DIVING DEEP ▲

Ospreys are not eagles but have life-styles similar to some of the fish-eating eagles. Like these eagles, ospreys regularly pluck fish from near the water's surface. But ospreys are the only ones that will dive deep to pursue their finny prey.

The huge harpy eagle is considered to be the world's most powerful bird.

CRUISING ►

Many eagles fly only about four to six hours each day. But the colorful bateleur takes to the skies early, gliding with its long, narrow wings for most of the day. Cruising over African plains at 35 to 50 miles per hour, it often covers 300 miles in a day.

OWLS

When the day-hunting raptors roost for the night, owls begin their hunt. On silent wings, they fly out in search of prey, using specialized senses—acute hearing and good night vision.

▲ A saw-whet owl catches a mouse.

FACE THE LIGHT▼

Most owls prefer to hunt in low light, either at dawn and dusk or throughout the night. But when owls have chicks to feed, they may hunt during the day as well. For some owls, such as the snowy owl (below), there is no choice. During the summer, snowy owls nesting in the Arctic have no nights in which to hunt!

BURROWING OWLS▲

Unlike most other owls, these unusual owls run well on the ground, form social groups, and live in burrows abandoned by ground squirrels or prairie dogs. When frightened, baby burrowing owls buzz like rattlesnakes, imitating these reptiles that also live in old burrows.

▲BIG & SMALL

Owls can be found on every continent except Antarctica. The largest is Europe's eagle owl (above), weighing in at six and a half pounds. The smallest, standing only about six inches tall, is the elf owl, found in the southwestern United States. It weighs slightly less than a golf ball.

◄ FISHY STORY

When fishing owls spot a fish near the water's surface, they swoop down to scoop it up, using long curved talons. Unlike other owls, fishing owls have featherless feet and legs—feathers would get too wet and messy.

FOOD FACTS

Unlike other raptors, owls do not eat carrion. Most owls prey on rodents. Smaller owls, such as the screech owl (right), feed on insects.

▲ BE VERY QUIET

The great gray owl will sometimes plunge into a smooth stretch of snow and come up with a mouse. Apparently, the owl can hear the rodents chewing in their tunnels beneath the surface. The barn owl and long-eared owl can hunt in complete darkness, using only their hearing to find prey.

VULTURES

As gruesome as they may seem, vultures play a very important role: They clean up. Without vultures, rotting carcasses would spread disease, not to mention stink up things! It is believed that vultures in Africa eat more meat than do all the other predators combined.

LET'S MEAT UP

Up to six kinds of vultures may gather at a large carcass in Africa. Large vultures, like the lappet-faced vulture (left), may be the only ones capable of ripping into the fresh carcass of a large animal, or eating tough parts such as bone and skin. Smaller vultures follow, eating the softer parts, sometimes climbing right inside a carcass to get at the meat.

◄ **BALD IS BEAUTIFUL**

It makes perfect sense that the king vulture has a bare head, because this carrion-eating bird sticks its head into gooey, rotting carcasses. After eating, most vultures enjoy a bath and will sometimes fly a great distance to find water.

LIKE A STORK?

Unlike their Old World relatives, vultures in the Americas, such as these black vultures, are more closely related to storks than to birds of prey. They have a keen sense of smell, while Old World vultures rely on sight and can locate food only in open country.

BONE DROP▼

Bearded vultures, or lammergeiers, prefer to eat bones. Small bones are swallowed whole, but bigger ones pose a problem. So bearded vultures carry the bones into the sky, as high up as 200 feet, then drop them onto the rocks below, breaking them into edible bits. The vultures employ the same strategy with tortoises.

EGGS- ▶ ACTLY

Egyptian vultures like to eat ostrich eggs, and they crack them open in a very interesting way. Small eggs are just picked up and thrown down. When eggs are too big to pick up, the vultures pick up stones and throw them until the eggs break—one of the few examples of tool use by an animal.

▼SMELL THAT?

The turkey vulture has an exceptionally good sense of smell, and can find carrion hidden beneath the rainforest canopy. It can tell the difference between edible meat and stuff that has become too rotten even for a vulture.

PEOPLE & BIRDS OF PREY

At first we treated raptors with respect, telling stories about their magic powers. Then we began to hunt them, often for no reason at all. About 50 years ago, we started using a lot of chemicals on the land that caused raptors to have trouble laying eggs that would hatch. But then we began to value birds of prey, and we started working to help them survive.

This golden eagle takes an up-close look at some fascinating school children.

▲ FARMER'S FRIEND

Golden eagles, such as the one above, are a big help to ranchers. They prey on rabbits and ground squirrels, which eat a lot of grass meant for sheep and cattle. Grain farmers should be happy to see hawks, because hawks hunt mice that eat the grain.

HUNTING TOGETHER

The sport of falconry—using a trained bird of prey to hunt game—is probably about 4,000 years old. Today, many falconers are involved in raptor conservation. In the U.S., they are legally allowed to use some species of raptors from the wild. They also continue to breed many raptor species in captivity for use in falconry.

GOOD CHANGE

Hawk Mountain, Pennsylvania, sits on a major flyway for migrating birds of prey. Hunters used to go there to shoot hawks passing overhead. Now Hawk Mountain is a sanctuary where bird watchers gather to see the almost 20,000 raptors that pass through each fall.

POWERFUL PLUMES

Most North American Indians used bald eagle and golden eagle feathers for religious and ceremonial purposes. Today, when one of these protected birds of prey is found dead, a government agency may give the feathers to a group of Native Americans.

IN TROUBLE

Many of the most endangered birds of prey, such as northern spotted owls, are in trouble because their habitat is disappearing. Other raptors have been hunted or poisoned. The California condor (left), the largest raptor in North America, is one of the rarest animals on earth. Fewer than one hundred California condors are living today.

▼RAPTOR REHAB

Injured birds of prey are cared for at raptor centers around the world. Birds that can fly and hunt are released back into the wild. Those that are unable to catch prey are cared for in captivity, and are often used to educate people about birds of prey.

▼LENDING A HAND

Scientists sometimes raise raptor chicks to release into wild areas that would make good homes. Because scientists don't want the birds to associate humans with food, the caretakers feed the chicks using a hand puppet shaped like an adult eagle's head.

Glossary

Bird of prey: Meat-eating birds that use their strong feet, talons, and hooked beak to catch and kill prey.

Cache: A hiding place used by animals to store food. Most falcons cache, or store, food, which gives them a food reserve when prey is scarce.

Canopy: The top layer of a forest. The thick canopy of the rain forest is made up of the branches of trees.

Carcass: The dead body of an animal.

Carrion: The rotting flesh of a dead animal.

Defensive display: A defense behavior in which a raptor fluffs up feathers on its head and body, raises its wings, hisses, clacks its beak, and opens its eyes very wide in order to make itself look bigger.

Diurnal: Active during the day. Most raptors are diurnal hunters.

Down: The covering of soft fluffy feathers on a baby bird.

Endangered: Threatened with extinction. The California condor is in danger of becoming extinct (dying out).

Falconry: The sport of hunting small birds and animals with trained raptors.

Ferruginous: Rust-colored. Ferruginous hawks have orange-red feathers.

Fledgling: A young bird. Fledglings are in the process of growing their adult feathers and training to leave the nest and hunt for themselves.

Gizzard: Part of a bird's stomach that contracts around unchewed food, breaks it down, and digests it.

Habitat: The place where an animal or plant naturally lives and grows.

Kiting: Hovering over one spot.

Migration: An animal's move away from or to its breeding grounds at certain times of year.

Molt: To shed skin, feathers, hair, or a shell. Eagles molt their downy feathers just weeks after hatching.

Nocturnal: Active at night. Most owls are nocturnal hunters.

Predator: An animal that hunts other animals for food.

Prey: An animal that is hunted by other animals for food.

Rain forest: A tropical woodland that averages 100 inches of rain a year.

Raptor: A bird of prey, such as an owl or hawk.

Rodent: A small mammal with sharp teeth such as a mouse, squirrel, or rabbit.

Sanctuary: An area established for the protection of animals or natural resources.

Savanna: A grassy plain with few or no trees.

Scavenger: An animal, such as a vulture, that feeds on dead rather than live animals.

Spawn: To produce eggs. A female fish places her eggs in the water, and the male fertilizes them.

Specialized: Adapted for a particular habitat, style of hunting, or climate.

Talon: The sharp curving claw of a bird of prey.

Thermal: A rising body of warm air on which birds can soar.

Transparent: Fine or thin enough to be seen through.

Vole: A small rodent that resembles a fat mouse and lives in meadows and mountainous areas.

Wingspan: The distance from the tip of one wing to the tip of the other wing.